Dahl-Jensen™
Porcelain Figurines
1897 - 1985

Caroline and Nick Pope

4880 Lower Valley Road, Atglen, PA 19310 USA

Dedication

To Else & Anker Dahl-Jensen

Library of Congress Cataloging-in-Publication Data:

Pope, Caroline.
     Dahl-Jensen porcelain figurines 1897-1985/by Caroline and Nick Pope.
     p. cm.
   ISBN 0-7643-1760-1 (Hardcover)
1. Dahl-Jensen, Jens Peter, 1874-1960. 2. Bing & Grondahl. 3. Porcelain figures—Denmark—History—20th century. I. Pope, Nick. II. Title.
NK4210.D23 A4 2003
738.8'2'0948913—dc21

                                        2002154629

Designed by John P. Cheek
Type set in Windsor BT/Korinna BT

ISBN: 0-7643-1760-1
Printed in China
1 2 3 4

Published by Schiffer Publishing Ltd.
4880 Lower Valley Road
Atglen, PA 19310
Phone: (610) 593-1777; Fax: (610) 593-2002
E-mail: Schifferbk@aol.com
Please visit our web site catalog at
www.schifferbooks.com
We are always looking for people to write books on new and related subjects. If you have an idea for a book, please contact us at the above address.

This book may be purchased from the publisher.
Include $3.95 for shipping. Please try your bookstore first.
You may write for a free catalog.

In Europe, Schiffer books are distributed by
Bushwood Books
6 Marksbury Ave. Kew Gardens
Surrey TW9 4JF England
Phone: 44 (0)20 8392-8585; Fax: 44 (0)20 8392-9876
E-mail: Bushwd@aol.com
Free postage in the UK. Europe: air mail at cost.
Please try your bookstore first.

Foreword by Else Dahl-Jensen

(granddaughter of Jens Peter Dahl-Jensen)

Dahl-Jensen Porcelain was founded as a small family firm in 1925. As the years passed an extensive collection of models was developed. Production was, nevertheless, limited as the family uncompromisingly sought to achieve quality through craftsmanship.

Emphasis on colour, in addition to form, was also an essential aspect. Through years of patient innovation those warm, golden colours and lively expressions so characteristic of the models were gradually realized.

My brother, Anker and I were privileged to be born into this creative milieu. At that time the family lived and worked together on a 200 year old farm, with extensive gardens, located in the village of Bronshoj on the outskirts of Copenhagen. Our real world became one where artists, loyal employees and customers came together as a unique community.

Both of us were fortunate to participate first as child and later as adult models for our grandfather: an energetic artist and sculptor. Unbeknownst to us at that time, we were later to offer 30 wonderful years of our lives to continue the family's dedication to porcelain.

Acknowledgments

With thanks to:

Margaret, Dave, Rebecca, and Charlotte.

Betty, John, Melissa Delson, Beatrix Forbes Fine Porcelain, Malcolm & Joan Floyde, Tom & Mabel Hood, Jane the Dane, D.M. Joos de ter Beerst, Kim Hauser, Kristi, Mark Potterton, Stan Tillotson (*www.stan.tillotson.com*), 'Teddies', Tom, Sylvia, and 'Wiffle', Ian Williams, Willi and Rosi, and the many other dealers and collectors from around the world who have helped us along the way. Special thanks go to Linda H. Purbaugh for her photographs of pieces from the collection of Lawrence E. Rubin.

En særlig tak rettes til vore danske venner, handlende såvel som samlere og her skal specielt nævnes - Christian Geisler, Lise Jahn, Ira Hartogsohn, Borg Jensen, Gunnar Jakobsen, Ulla Kayser, Klaus Madsen, Mogens, Peter, Jan Ringsmose, P R Monter (*www.pr.dk*), DPH Trading (*www.dph-trading.dk*).

We have received significant assistance from the family of Jens Peter Dahl-Jensen, without which this book would be significantly less accurate and complete. In particular, we acknowledge their kind permission to reproduce images from a stock catalog which remains the copyright of the Dahl-Jensen family.

Contents

Introduction

To many collectors the Danish porcelain industry starts and ends with the Royal factory but many do not appreciate that the industry was far more wide ranging with a number of factories producing porcelain of high quality both so far as artistic merit and manufacturing techniques are concerned.

Bing & Grondahl produced a vast range of products many of which were designed or sculpted by artists who also worked for Royal Copenhagen. Pre-eminent amongst these was Jens Peter Dahl-Jensen who subsequently set up his own factory assisted by his son Georg.

We therefore originally decided it would be useful to produce a book on Bing & Grondahl but to provide within it a significant section on Dahl-Jensen as the two are so intimately linked. However the amount of information made it impossible to confine it to a single volume and with the help of the Dahl-Jensen family a separate book became a viable option.

We have indicated in the listing interesting similarities in subject, style or technique between pieces sculpted by Dahl-Jensen for both factories. We have also indicated similarities between the Danish porcelain producers and sculptors, for instance Lauritz Jensen worked either directly or on commission for all three factories.

Though it should be appreciated that there is little information available on the work of individual sculptors for the Bing & Grondahl factory we have endeavored to make attributions where possible. We have been able to definitely attribute over 70 pieces sculpted by Dahl-Jensen for Bing & Grondahl but we have refrained from making guesses purely on style and subject matter even when the style is virtually unmistakable.

The Dahl-Jensen Factory
A Short History

Jens Peter Dahl-Jensen was born on July 23rd 1874 in the small town of Nibe in Jutland the son of a cabinet maker. He became apprenticed to a joiner in Aalborg at the same time learning the cabinet maker and wood-carver's trade and this aroused his interest in modeling. He soon realized the art of sculpture was his field of work producing animals in wood and also making furniture for himself and his family. At this time he signed his work 'Jens Jensen' and it was some time later that he decided to use his full name instead.

After attending the Technical College in Aalborg he was awarded a silver medal for his journeyman's probation work. The result was the opportunity to study at the Royal Academy of Arts in Copenhagen from 1894 to 1897.

At the same time taking lessons from Vilhelm Bissen – a master in the art of sculpture of the time. When the Academy was closed during the summer Dahl-Jensen would study in Berlin and Dresden, and after his final exams at the Royal Academy he went on to Switzerland and Italy for further education.

In 1900 Dahl-Jensen had married a porcelain painter who since the age of 14 had been working first at the Royal Copenhagen Porcelain Factory and then at Bing & Grondahl.

On his return from abroad he was appointed sculptor at the Bing & Grondahl Factory where he worked until 1917 producing many fine sculptures mainly of animals sculpted from life in the adjacent city zoo. He was such a familiar figure in his distinctive hat that it is said the animals responded to him.

From 1917 to 1925 Dahl-Jensen was the manager of the Bing & Grondahl's Norden porcelain factory. It seems that this position was not one he had sought and he found little personal or artistic challenge when required to perform it.

Whilst working at the factory during the day Dahl-Jensen would work in his studio at home in the evenings where he modeled a series of beasts of prey. These were cast in bronze which he chiseled himself but some of which later formed the basis of his factory produced collection.

These bronze figures were exhibited every year at The Royal Academy of Arts at Charlottenborg, other Danish exhibitions or abroad such as Malmo – Berlin – Munchen and San Francisco between 1901 and 1925.

Late in 1924 whilst visiting his son Georg who had himself set up a small porcelain factory in Italy for a Venetian glass works, Dahl-Jensen decided it would be possible to set up a small factory himself.

With Georg's help a suitable building at 288 Frederikssundsvej in the north-western outskirts of Copenhagen was acquired on 25th August 1925.

Then began the rebuilding work necessary to produce porcelain. The most important part was to construct a moderate size kiln which proved difficult and during the first year most firings failed.

After nearly two years they succeeded in producing porcelain of an acceptable quality and not only produced underglaze decorated figures but also 'crackle' glaze vases, bowls and bowls with lids. Much of the crackle glaze porcelain was decorated by Dahl-Jensen's daughter-in-law Christa.

In the beginning sales where mainly to the USA followed by Danish shops and then other countries.

Dahl-Jensen modeled new sculptures creating a series of figures representing models from the Far East based on models and costumes of touring entertainers passing through Copenhagen who would come to the factory to pose during the day and leaving to perform in the evening.

Production steadily increased and it was then possible to acquire the works of other artists to enlarge the model collection. Of the almost 400 figurines the factory produced Dahl-Jensen himself sculpted about 280.

As time passed Dahl-Jensen and his son where joined by his grand-daughter Else as a painter and his grand-son Anker on the technical side in preparation for them taking on the running of the factory.

Factory mark with Else Dahl-Jensen's monogram

Dahl-Jensen's life dream became a reality when he was able to reproduce his own works himself so that many others might enjoy them. Even at the height of production there were no more than 40 workers employed in a factory more like a family than a business and many workers are still in touch with the family.

Jens Peter Dahl-Jensen died on December 12 1960 aged 86 working almost until the end. The factory closed in 1985 but his work is still to be found on the second hand market and is greatly admired throughout the world.

Much of the information above was taken from an article about Dahl-Jensen by his son Georg reproduced with the kind permission of his grandchildren Else and Anker who also provided personal reminiscences.

Jens Peter Dahl-Jensen pictured with his hat, as featured in piece number 1244, which is a self portrait of Laurits Jensen wearing it.

Portrait of Dahl-Jensen featuring pieces 1209 and 1211 (reproduced with permission of Else Dahl-Jensen)

Jens Peter Dahl-Jensen, 1944, aged 70.

Factory Marks

As far as we know only three factory marks were used.

Pre-1928 factory mark

Post-1928 factory mark

Date unknown, possibly used on items other than figurines i.e. vases etc.

A 'second' with a vertical scratch through the crown.

A 'second,' with scratch through the crown.

A 'third' with vertical and horizontal scratches through the crown. See 1023 Pomona.

Materials and Techniques

Listed below are some of the types of wares and decorative finishes produced by the factory with brief descriptions to aid identification.

Porcelain

Hard paste porcelain originated in China but it was not until the middle of the 18th century that European chemists were able to duplicate the quality which the Chinese had been producing for hundreds of years. The particular feature is the high temperature at which the porcelain is fired (around 900°C for first firing and 1440°C during glazing).

Stoneware is gray clay rather than white and the temperature at which it is first fired is higher (1250°C) but after glazing is lower (900 °C) and so a wider range of colors can be used under the glaze.

Underglaze Decoration

The porcelain is allowed to dry after casting and then decorated by hand. After painting the piece is covered with an opaque layer which melts in the final firing to become clear. The pigments used only show their color after firing and decorators have to be extremely skilled as they cannot see shades of color which depend on the thickness of the pigment. Originally only blue was used but then red and green were added followed by gray and brown. It will be seen that an extraordinary range of colors and effects can be achieved. As all the figurines are hand painted there can be considerable variations in finish. Generally the stronger colors seem to be in most demand.

Blanc de Chine

A porcelain with a special glaze which appears to be pure white.

Cracquelé

First produced in 1910 and perfected about 1920 by C F Ludvigsen at the Royal factory it is produced by allowing for different rates of shrinkage during the second firing resulting in a network of cracks being formed during cooling. Then color is applied into the cracks and a further protective glaze applied.

Seconds (or worse)

Sometimes the factory failed to produce perfection and pieces were marked as 'seconds'. This was done by scratching through the factory mark either with a diamond cutter or a wheel, usually horizontal but sometimes vertical. There are also thirds. From our experience in looking at many seconds beauty is in the eye of the beholder. The reasons why some pieces are seconds are sometimes unclear ranging from minor color variation from the norm to obvious blemishes.

Whether to buy a second is a personal matter and some collectors will not tolerate seconds (we have a number of seconds, thirds and fourths).

Support (Pontil) marks

Some of the larger pieces require additional support during firing resulting in small circular marks beneath the supported area. It is not possible to eliminate the color variation caused thus leaving a mark which, in our opinion does not detract from attractiveness or value.

Glazing flaws

Porcelain is fired at very high temperatures and dark glazes on older pieces tend to be prone to firing defects particularly to eyes. We feel small glazing flaws are to be expected on pieces over 80 years old.

Damage/Restoration

As restoration techniques are improving all the time it is more and more difficult to detect restoration to high glaze porcelain pieces. Use of black (ultra violet) light can help but we have been deceived and feel that the best method of detection is touch.

There is no reason to refuse to buy a restored piece provided the price is right and you like it.

List by Sculptors

The Dahl-Jensen company, like the Bing & Grondahl factory, bought or commissioned pieces from a number of well known sculptors. We have attributed those pieces, where we can, to the following sculptors.

**Dahl-Jensen, Jens Peter
(1874-1960)**

Dahl Jensen	*DP.*

1001	Wire-haired Fox Terrier
1002	Sealyham standing
1003	Pekinese sitting
1004	Diamond Terrier
1005	Cat
1006	Diamond Terrier
1007	Girl in nightdress
1008	Sealyham puppy sitting
1009	Wire-haired Fox Terrier standing
1010	Mouse sitting
1011	Card tray with white mice
1012	Mouse lying
1013	Kitten
1014	Serval
1015	Lynx - white
1017	Bear, brown
1018	Orang-utan standing
1019	Puma sitting
1020	Panther
1021	Hen
1022	Lion lying
1024	Great Lynx
1025	Desert Lynx
1026	'Gutte'
1027	Boy with pipe
1028	Sea Scorpion
1029	Duckling
1030	Shrike
1031	Wren
1032	Duckling outspread wings
1036	Boy with anchor
1040	Boy wearing cap
1041	Polar Lynx

1048	Blue Titmouse
1049	Kingfisher
1050	Crested Tit
1051	Cockatoo
1052	Bullfinch
1053	African Rockhen
1058	Elephant
1064	Boy in winter clothes
1065	Basset Hound puppy
1066	Scottish Terrier
1069	'Deadly Boxer'
1072	Boy with terrier
1074	Brussels Griffon
1075	Papillon
1076	Bedlington Terrier
1077	Wire Fox Terrier
1078	Scottish Terrier sitting
1079	Airedale Terrier
1080	Kerry Blue Terrier
1081	Lynx - hissing
1082	Greenland Hound
1083	Turkey cock
1084	German Shepherd lying
1085	Girl hugging Wire Fox Terrier
1086	Monkey on rock
1087	German Shepherd standing
1088	French Bulldog sitting
1089	Dancing Girl
1090	Mouse dancing
1094	Scottish Terrier sitting
1095	Schnauzer
1096	Boy reading
1098	French Bulldog puppy
1100	German Shepherd
1101	Penguin
1102	Skye Terrier - standing
1103	Skye Terrier - sitting
1104	Long Eared Owl
1105	Baby sitting
1106	Girl with doll

1107	Girl reading
1108	Cat
1109	Pekinese book end
1110	Amager girl - seated
1111	Great Dane seated
1112	Great Dane lying
1113	Elephant
1114	Javanese dancer
1115	Elephant
1116	Girl with a butterfly
1117	Girl from East - Sierra Leone
1118	Wire Fox Terrier
1119	Woman making ceramics
1120	Maltese Terrier
1122	Bear on rock
1123	Egyptian woman
1124	Spanish dancer
1125	Siamese temple dancer
1128	Great Dane
1129	Arabian girl
1130	German Shepherd
1131	Dachshund
1132	German Shepherd - sitting
1133	Cavalier King Charles Spaniel
1134	Pekinese puppy
1135	Bulldog
1136	Bali woman
1137	Borzoi
1138	Polar bear
1139	Bulldog puppy
1140	Hare standing
1141	Hare sitting
1142	Girl from Hedebo (2 versions)
1143	Borzoi
1144	Girl from Havdrup
1145	Cocker Spaniel
1146	Pekinese
1147	Deer (doe)
1148	Pomeranian
1149	Cairn Terrier

1150	Girl from Skovshoved	1225	Sailor boy	1319	Tern
1151	Girl with pail	1226	Indian flame dancer	1320	Warbler
1152	Girl with teddy	1228	Boy with carrot	1321	House Martin
1153	Oriental flute player	1229	Indian bust	1322	Aju Sitra (dancer)
1154	Man with accordion	1230	Sparrow	1323	'Monuia'
1155	Geisha playing instrument	1232	Goldfinch	1324	Bridesmaid from Fano
1156	Polar bear	1233	Long-tailed Tit	1325	Fano woman
1157	Polar bear - sitting	1234	Cow lying	1326	Japanese juggler
1158	Girl with Christmas goat	1236	Desert Fox	1327	Children with picture book
1159	Japanese woman	1237	Antelope	1328	'Ole'
1160	'Psyche'	1238	Oriental fruit seller	1329	Cat
1161	Cupid with ball	1239	Kinglet	1330	Ferret
1162	Cupid playing with foot	1240	Pied Flycatcher	1331	Ferret
1163	Cupid with rose	1241	Brambling	1332	'Ellen'
1164	'Cupid & Psyche'	1242	Redstart	1333	Chamois
1165	Girl from Fano	1243	Waxwing	1334	Faun with oil lamp
1166	Boy with car	1246	Tiger sitting	1335	Ballerina
1167	Boy with blocks	1247	Blue Warbler	1336	Faun with wine bottle
1168	Nude	1248	Wagtail	1337	Pekinese
1169	Pekinese	1249	Chaffinch	1338	Ballerina
1170	Boxer	1250	American Kinglet	1339	Polar bear cubs
1171	Javanese Princess	1251	Woman's head	1340	Dachshund
1180	Girl with snowball	1253	'Evening Prayer'	1341	Mermaid
1186	English Setter sitting	1254	Moroccan dancer	1342	Merman on rock
1187	English Setter lying	1260	Indonesian Temple Dancer	1343	Woodpecker
1188	Carpenter	1268	Hawaiian girl with bird	1344	Bear cubs
1189	Bricklayer	1269	Madonna & Child	1345	Kookaburra
1190	Baker	1270	Boy with mouse	1346	Bear cub
1191	Blacksmith	1277	'Ida'	1347	Bear cub
1192	Chimneysweep	1279	Peewit	1348	Flycatcher
1193	Paver (construction)	1280	Robin	1349	Bird on a nest
1194	Fisherman	1281	Duck	1350	Girl from Egtved (costume
1195	Butcher	1287	Girl with an apple basket		from the Bronze Age)
1196	Boy eating sausages	1288	Girl with apple branch	1352	Oriental dancer
1197	Girl knitting	1289	'Etude'	1353	Girl selling pearls
1204	Girl with toy elephant	1291	Boy with cat	1355	Rose breasted crossbill
1205	Boy with top	1292	Pompeiian dancer	1356	Crossbill
1206	Schnauzer with boy on base	1293	Spanish dancers	1357	Jay
1207	'Else'	1294	Fisherboy	1358	Greenland boy kneeling
1208	Sumatra dancer	1295	'Bente'	1359	Japanese girl
1209	Girl from Frederiksborg	1296	Goosegirl	1360	Berber girl
1210	Girl from Aalborg	1297	Princess with fan	1361	Gull
1211	Bust of African woman	1298	Prince & Princess	1362	American Indian bust
1212	Lady reclining on chaise	1299	Snake charmer	1363	Geese
	longue (2 versions)	1300	Amager boy with pipe	1364	Goose
1213	Girl with dog and bone	1301	Girl with vegetables	1365	'Tine'
1214	Boy & girl & boat	1304	Cocker Spaniel	1367	Mallard
1215	'Evening Sun'	1305	Sudanese man with cockatoo	1368	Duckling
1216	'Morning Sun'	1308	Budgerigar	1369	Duckling
1217	'Greta'	1309	'Flora'	1370	Duckling
1218	Boy with trumpet	1310	Polar bear (walking)	1371	Duckling
1219	'Hanne' - 2 versions	1311	Kris fighter	1372	Duckling
1220	'Proposal'	1312	'The dream'	1375	Perch
1221	Oriental dancer	1314	Cuckoo	1376	Sea Roach
1222	Boy - seated	1315	Australian Wren	1377	Sea Scorpion
1223	Girl - seated	1316	Cockatoo	1378	Schoolgirl from Sweden
1224	Ballerina with mirror	1318	Seagull	1380	Sealion

1381	Seal
1382	Sprat
1383	Crucian Carp
1384	Redfish
1385	Sea Roach
1386	Great Redfish
1388	Codfish

Andersen, Herman
1174 Girl with apple

Andersen, Vilhelm
1121 Ermine on log

Bonnesen, Carl Johan
(1868 – 1933)

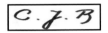

1055	Chimpanzee
1056	Elephant - African
1057	Elephant - Indian
1059	Elephant with calf
1060	Bear lying on back with 2 cubs playing
1067	Polar bear
1068	Polar bear & cubs
1126	Polar bear
1127	Cat sitting
1231	Rhinoceros
1252	French workhorse

Bregno, Jens Jakob

1172	Girl with mandolin
1173	Faun with grapes
1175	'Spring'
1176	Faun & woman
1177	'Morning'
1178	'Eva '
1179	'Hercules'
1181	Mother & baby
1182	'Susanne'
1183	'Thor'
1184	'Paradise'
1185	Thor
1198	Faun with ducklings
1199	'The Elevation'
1200	'Susanne's Sister'
1201	'Jacob's Fight'
1202	Adam and Eve
1203	'Regnar Lodbrog'

Christensen, Georg
1091	Chinese on pillow
1092	Mermaid
1093	Girl on stool

Dorlit, Helge
1373	Hunter with dog
1374	Goat
1389	Perched Owl
1390	Snowy Owl

Galster, Johan

| 1392 | 'Lisa' |

Jensen, Lauritz

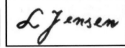

1235	Pointer lying
1244	Sculptor (self portrait)
1245	Boy with sail boat
1255	Broholmer puppy
1256	Buffalo lying
1257	Dachshunds playing
1258	Wolf howling
1259	Lion & lioness
1261	American Indian on horse
1262	Girl with cow
1263	Lion roaring
1264	Fresian bull
1265	Deer
1266	Cowboy on horse
1267	Deer with fawn
1271	Wounded Soldier with horse
1272	Polar bear with fish
1273	Bull goring tiger
1274	Lion cubs - pair
1275	Lion cub
1276	Woman with fawn (on base)
1278	English Setters on base
1282	Irish Setter on base
1283	German Shorthair Pointer on base
1284	Refugees
1285	Tiger with haunch
1286	Lion roaring
1290	Osprey with fish
1302	Bull
1391	Bull

Jorgensen, Borge
| 1351 | 'Lene' |

| 1354 | 'Jette' |
| 1366 | 'Anne' |

Lemser, Poul
1034	'Venus & Cupid'
1035	Faun with grapes
1037	'Leda & Swan'
1038	Faun with baby
1039	Faun & nymph
1042	Bonbon dish with figurine
1043	Bottle with figurine
1044	Girl with pigeon
1046	Boy with duck
1070	'Hans Clodhopper'
1071	'Emperors New Clothes'

Madsen, Aug. Svejstrup

1045	Rabbit
1054	Duckling
1073	Penguin

Mathiesen, Emma
1097 Choirboy

Nielsen, Erling Vangedal

| 1379 | Salmon |
| 1387 | Trout |

Nordstrom, Patrick
1047 Girl with fish

Osterbye, Inger
1227 Greenlander with baby

Roerup, Linda
1303	Brother & sister
1306	Girl with roller-skates
1307	Tea girl
1313	Woman with 3 pigs
1317	Gypsy woman

Wahlstedt, Viola
1016	Woman with fish
1023	Pomona
1033	Woman with agave
1099	Girl on a shell

List by Category

Birds

Bird of Prey
1290 Osprey with fish

Exotic Birds
1051 Cockatoo
1053 African Rockhen
1308 Budgerigar
1316 Cockatoo
1345 Kookaburra

Garden Birds
1031 Wren
1048 Blue Titmouse
1050 Crested Tit
1052 Bullfinch
1230 Sparrow
1232 Goldfinch
1233 Long-tailed Tit
1240 Pied Flycatcher
1241 Brambling
1242 Redstart
1248 Wagtail
1249 Chaffinch
1279 Peewit
1280 Robin
1320 Warbler
1321 House Martin
1348 Flycatcher
1349 Bird on a nest
1355 Rose breasted crossbill
1356 Crossbill

Owls
1104 Long Eared Owl
1389 Perched Owl
1390 Snowy Owl

Penguins
1073 Penguin
1101 Penguin

Sea Birds
1318 Seagull
1319 Tern
1361 Gull

Water Birds
1029 Duckling
1032 Duckling outspread wings
1049 Kingfisher
1054 Duckling
1281 Duck
1363 Geese
1364 Goose
1367 Mallard
1368 Duckling
1369 Duckling
1370 Duckling
1371 Duckling
1372 Duckling

Wild Birds
1030 Shrike
1239 Kinglet
1243 Waxwing
1247 Blue Warbler
1250 American Kinglet
1314 Cuckoo
1315 Australian Wren
1343 Woodpecker
1357 Jay

Cats
1005 Cat
1108 Cat
1013 Kitten
1127 Cat sitting
1329 Cat

Dogs

Gun Dogs
1133 Cavalier King Charles Spaniel
1145 Cocker Spaniel
1186 English Setter sitting
1187 English Setter lying
1235 Pointer lying
1278 English Setters on base
1282 Irish Setter on base
1283 German Shorthair Pointer on base
1304 Cocker Spaniel

Hounds
1065 Basset Hound puppy
1082 Greenland Hound
1131 Dachshund
1137 Borzoi
1143 Borzoi
1255 Broholmer puppy
1257 Dachshunds playing
1340 Dachshund

Terriers
1001 Wire-haired Fox Terrier
1002 Sealyham standing
1008 Sealyham puppy sitting
1009 Wire-haired Fox Terrier standing
1066 Scottish Terrier
1076 Bedlington Terrier
1077 Wire Fox Terrier
1078 Scottish Terrier sitting
1079 Airedale Terrier
1080 Kerry Blue Terrier
1094 Scottish Terrier sitting
1102 Skye Terrier - standing
1103 Skye Terrier - sitting
1118 Wire Fox Terrier
1120 Maltese Terrier
1149 Cairn Terrier

Toy Dogs
1003 Pekinese sitting
1004 Diamond Terrier standing

1006	Diamond Terrier sitting
1074	Brussels Griffon
1075	Papillon
1134	Pekinese puppy
1146	Pekinese
1148	Pomeranian
1169	Pekinese
1337	Pekinese

Utility Dogs

1088	French Bulldog sitting
1095	Schnauzer
1098	French Bulldog puppy
1135	Bulldog
1139	Bulldog puppy

Working Dogs

1084	German Shepherd lying
1087	German Shepherd standing
1100	German Shepherd
1109	Pekinese, book end
1111	Great Dane seated
1112	Great Dane lying
1128	Great Dane
1130	German Shepherd
1132	German Shepherd - sitting
1170	Boxer
1206	Schnauzer with boy on base

Farm/Domestic Animals

Bulls/Cow

1264	Friesian bull
1273	Bull goring tiger
1302	Bull
1391	Bull
1234	Cow lying

Horse

| 1252 | French workhorse |

Fowl

| 1021 | Hen |
| 1083 | Turkey cock |

Figurines

Adult & Child

| 1181 | Mother & baby |

Busts

1211	Bust of African woman
1229	Indian bust
1251	Woman's head
1362	American Indian bust
1365	'Tine'

Children

1007	Girl in nightdress
1026	'Gutte'
1027	Boy with pipe
1033	Woman with agave
1036	Boy with anchor
1040	Boy wearing cap
1044	Little girl with pigeon
1046	Boy with duck
1047	Girl with fish
1064	Boy in winter clothes
1069	'Deadly Boxer'
1072	Boy with terrier
1085	Girl hugging Wire Fox Terrier
1089	Dancing Girl
1093	Girl on stool
1096	Boy reading
1097	Choirboy
1099	Girl on a shell
1105	Baby sitting
1106	Girl with doll
1107	Girl reading
1116	Girl with a butterfly
1151	Girl with pail
1152	Girl with teddy
1158	Girl with Christmas goat
1166	Boy with car
1167	Boy with blocks
1172	Girl with mandolin
1174	Girl with apple
1180	Girl with snowball
1196	Boy eating sausages
1197	Girl knitting
1204	Girl with toy elephant
1205	Boy with top
1207	'Else'
1213	Girl with dog and bone
1214	Boy & girl & boat
1215	'Evening Sun'
1216	'Morning Sun'
1217	'Greta'
1218	Boy with trumpet
1219	'Hanne' - 2 versions
1222	Seated boy
1223	Seated girl
1225	Sailor boy
1228	Boy with carrot
1245	Boy with sail boat
1270	Boy with mouse
1277	'Ida'
1287	Girl with an apple basket

1288	Girl with apple branch
1291	Boy with cat
1294	Fisherboy
1295	'Bente'
1303	Brother & sister
1306	Girl with roller-skates
1309	'Flora'
1327	Children with picture book
1328	'Ole'
1332	'Ellen'
1351	'Lene'
1354	'Jette'
1366	'Anne'
1392	'Lisa'

Laurits Jensen

| 1244 | Sculptor (self portrait wearing Dahl-Jensen's distinctive hat) |

Exotic Figurines

1091	Chinese on pillow
1114	Javanese dancer
1117	Girl from East - Sierra Leone
1123	Egyptian woman
1124	Spanish dancer
1125	Siamese temple dancer
1129	Arabian girl
1136	Bali woman
1153	Oriental flute player
1155	Geisha playing instrument
1159	Japanese woman
1171	Javanese Princess
1177	'Morning'
1208	Sumatra dancer
1221	Oriental dancer
1226	Indian flame dancer
1238	Oriental fruit seller
1253	'Evening Prayer'
1254	Moroccan dancer
1260	Indonesian Temple Dancer
1268	Hawaiian girl with bird
1292	Pompeiian dancer
1293	Spanish dancers
1299	Snake charmer
1305	Sudanese man with cockatoo
1311	Kris fighter
1322	Aju Sitra (dancer)
1323	'Monuia'
1326	Japanese juggler
1352	Oriental dancer
1353	Girl selling pearls
1359	Japanese girl
1360	Berber girl
1307	Tea girl

Fairytale Characters
1070 'Hans Clodhopper'
1071 'Emperors New Clothes'
1297 Princess with fan
1298 Prince & Princess

Figurines
1199 'The Elevation'
1200 'Susanne's Sister'
1201 'Jacob's Flight'
1202 'Adam and Eve'
1220 'Proposal'
1261 American Indian on horse
1262 Girl with cow
1266 Cowboy on horse
1269 Madonna & Child
1271 Wounded soldier with horse
1284 Refugees
1317 Gypsy woman
1350 Girl from Egtved (costumed from the Bronze Age)
1373 Hunter with dog

Historical Figurines
1203 'Regnar Lodbrog'

Men
1154 Man with accordion

Mythical Figurines
1034 'Venus & Cupid'
1035 Faun with grapes
1037 'Leda & Swan'
1038 Faun with baby
1039 Faun & nymph
1092 Mermaid
1160 'Psyche'
1161 Cupid with ball
1162 Cupid playing with foot
1163 Cupid with rose
1164 'Cupid & Psyche'
1173 Faun with grapes
1175 'Spring'
1176 Faun & woman
1178 'Eva '
1179 'Hercules'
1182 'Susanne'
1183 'Thor'
1184 'Paradise'
1185 Thor
1198 Faun with ducklings
1334 Faun with oil lamp
1336 Faun with wine bottle
1341 Mermaid
1342 Merman on rock

Scandinavian Figurines
1378 Schoolgirl from Sweden
1110 Amager girl - seated
1142 Girl from Hedebo (2 versions)
1144 Girl from Havdrup
1150 Girl from Skovshoved
1165 Girl from Fano
1209 Girl from Frederiksborg
1210 Girl from Aalborg
1227 Greenlander with baby
1300 Amager boy with pipe
1324 Bridesmaid from Fano
1325 Fano woman
1358 Greenland boy kneeling

Women
1016 Woman with fish
1023 Pomona
1119 Woman making ceramics
1168 Nude
1212 Lady reclining on chaise longue (2 versions)
1224 Ballerina with mirror
1276 Woman with fawn (on base)
1289 'Etude'
1296 Goosegirl
1301 Girl with vegetables
1312 'The dream'
1313 Woman with 3 pigs
1335 Ballerina
1338 Ballerina

Workmen
1188 Carpenter
1189 Bricklayer
1190 Baker
1191 Blacksmith
1192 Chimneysweep
1193 Paver (construction)
1194 Fisherman
1195 Butcher

Dishes with Figurines
1042 Bonbon dish with figurine
1043 Bottle with figurine

Fish
1028 Sea Scorpion
1375 Perch
1376 Sea Roach
1377 Sea Scorpion
1379 Salmon
1382 Sprat
1383 Crucian Carp
1384 Redfish
1385 Sea Roach
1386 Great Redfish
1387 Trout
1388 Codfish

Rodents

Ermine/Ferrets
1121 Ermine on log
1330 Ferret
1331 Ferret

Hare/Rabbits
1045 Rabbit
1141 Hare
1140 Hare standing

Mice
1010 Mouse sitting
1011 Card tray with white mice
1012 Mouse lying
1090 Mouse dancing

Wild Animals

Antelope/Deer
1147 Deer (doe)
1237 Antelope
1265 Deer
1267 Deer with fawn
1333 Chamois
1374 Fawn

Bears
1017 Bear, brown
1344 Bear cubs
1346 Bear cub
1347 Bear cub
1060 Bear lying on back with 2 cubs playing
1122 Bear on rock

Buffalo
1256 Buffalo lying

Cat Family
1014 Serval
1015 Lynx, white
1019 Puma sitting
1020 Panther
1022 Lion lying
1024 Great Lynx
1025 Desert Lynx
1041 Polar Lynx

1081	Lynx - hissing
1246	Tiger sitting
1259	Lion & lioness
1263	Lion roaring
1273	Bull goring tiger
1274	Lion cubs - pair
1275	Lion cub
1285	Tiger with haunch
1286	Lion roaring

Elephants

1056	Elephant - African
1057	Elephant - Indian
1058	Elephant
1059	Elephant with calf
1113	Elephant

| 1115 | Elephant |

Fox

| 1236 | Desert Fox |

Polar Bears

1067	Polar bear
1068	Polar bear & cubs
1126	Polar bear
1138	Polar bear
1156	Polar bear
1157	Polar bear - sitting
1272	Polar bear with fish
1310	Polar bear (walking)
1339	Polar bear cubs

Primates

1018	Orang-utan standing
1055	Chimpanzee
1086	Monkey on rock

Rhinoceros

| 1231 | Rhinoceros |

Seal/Sealions

| 1381 | Seal |
| 1380 | Sealion |

Wolf

| 1258 | Wolf howling |

Illustrated Numerical List of Figurines by Jens Peter Dahl-Jensen

In this chapter the figures by Jens Peter Dahl-Jensen are listed in numerical order. The majority are underglaze decorated though some are stoneware or blanc de chine. Where possible comprehensive information has been given (see below) but in a number of cases the reference material gives only the barest detail. The information is provided in the following order:

Piece Number

Description – a simple description of the piece or the official Dahl-Jensen title.

Sculptor – all pieces sculpted by Dahl-Jensen unless otherwise indicated.

Size – a guide only can be given. Size can vary significantly on each piece during production. Where a single size is given this is normally the height unless the piece is wider than it is tall. All sizes are in centimeters.

Comments – observations and further information.

Value – in most cases a fairly wide range has been given because the factors affecting value can make significant differences. All prices are based on the piece being perfect. In particular age, quality of decoration and availability influence prices. Sale prices at collectors fairs, auctions and on the internet have been analyzed over a long period and prices for the same piece can vary by as much as 500%. In addition some subjects for instance dogs, cats, fish and fauns appeal to a wider market not limited to Danish porcelain collectors.

We have not included a guide to rarity, as all Dahl-Jensen is equally in demand and size or availability differentials are directly related to value.

1001
Wire-haired Fox Terrier
18cms
Compare Bing & Grondahl 1998
$250-$400

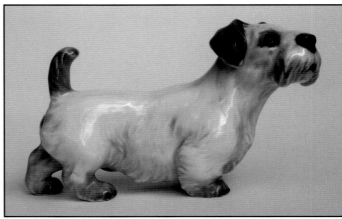

1002
Sealyham standing
17cms
$200-$350

1003
Pekinese sitting
13cms
Compare Bing & Grondahl 1631, 1637, 1986, and 1987
$200-$350

1004
Diamond Terrier standing
13.5cms
See 1006
$150-$250

1005
Cat
14cms
$75-$150

1006
Diamond Terrier sitting
13.5cms
See 1004
$100-$200

1007
Girl in nightdress
18.5cms
$175-$300

1008
Sealyham puppy sitting
12cms
Compare Bing & Grondahl
2027 and 2028
$150-$275

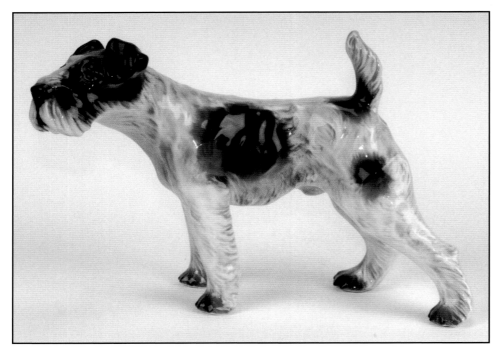

1009
Wire-haired Fox Terrier standing
21cms
$150-$275

1010
Mouse sitting
6cms
Compare Bing & Grondahl
1728 and 1801
$75-$150

1011
Card tray with white mice
20cms
Compare with Bing & Grondahl 1562
$225-$375

1012
Mouse lying
5.7cms
$75-$150

1013
Kitten
12.5cms
$75-$150

1014
Serval
24.5cms
$350-$600

1015
Lynx - white

1017
Bear, brown
24cms
See 1122 – size variation
$350-$600

1018
Orang-utan standing
20cms
$350-$500

1019
Puma sitting
30cms
Compare Bing & Grondahl 1584 and 1993
$550-$800

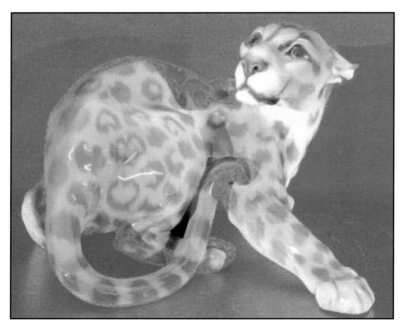

1020
Lynx
23.5cms
Compare Bing & Grondahl 1613
$600-$850

1021
Hen
16cms
$300-$425

1022
Lion lying
36.5cms
$950-$1,350

1024
Great Lynx
28cms
$750-$950

1025
Desert Lynx
23cms
Also available
without a base
$400-$700

1026
'Gutte'
18.5cms
$250-$375

1027
Boy with pipe
15.5cms
$225-$350

1028
Sea Scorpion
11.5cms
$350-$450

1029
Duckling
8cms
Compare Bing & Grondahl 1548
$75-$125

1030
Shrike
14.5cms
Compare to B&G 1633 and Royal Copenhagen 410
$150-$250

1031
Wren
6.5cms
$75-$125

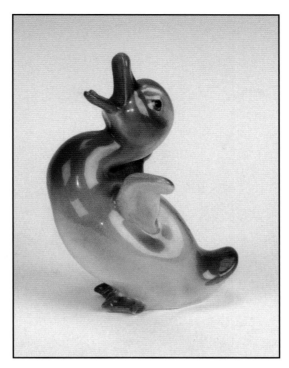

1032
Duckling outspread wings
11.5cms
$125-$200

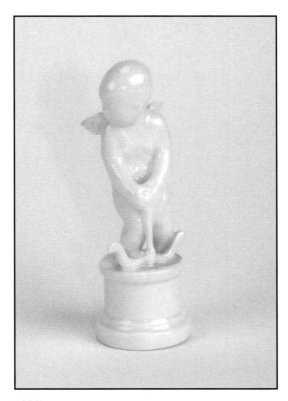

1036
Boy with anchor
Blanc de chine
$125-$200

1040
Boy wearing cap
10cms
$225-$350

1041
Polar Lynx
21.5cms
$400-$600

1048
Blue Titmouse
8.5cms
$100-$200

1049
Kingfisher
14.5cms
Compare Bing & Grondahl 1619
$175-$250

1051
Cockatoo
24cms
$300-$550

1050
Crested Tit
10.5cms
Compare Bing & Grondahl 1675
$125-$225

1052
Bullfinch
10.5cms
$150-$275

1053
African Rockhen
12cms
$100-$200

1058
Elephant
12cms
$200-$300

1061
Unknown

1062
Unknown

1063
Unknown

1064
Boy in winter clothes
19.5cms
$200-$300

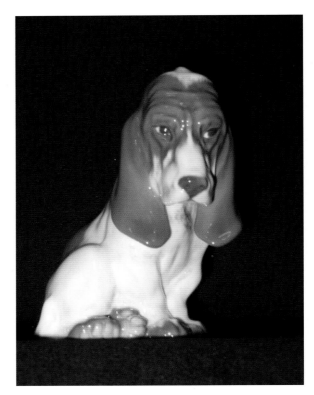

1065
Basset Hound puppy
14.5cms
$100-$200

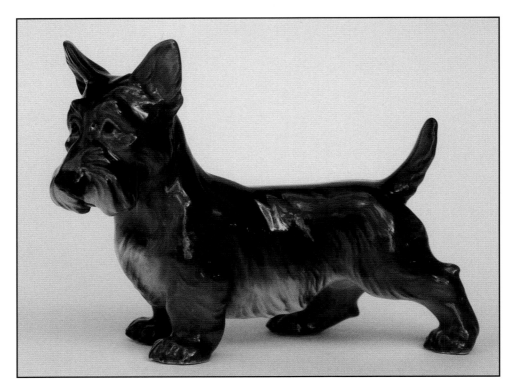

1066
Scottish Terrier
17cms
$100-$200

1069
'Deadly Boxer'
14.5cms
$150-$250

1072
Boy with terrier
32.5cms
$850-$1,100

1074
Brussels Griffon
10cms
$125-$300

1075
Papillon
11cms
$125-$300

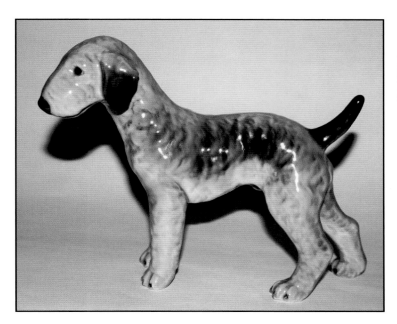

1076
Bedlington Terrier
19.5cms
$150-$350

1077
Wire Haired Fox Terrier sitting
16cms
$150-$300

1078
Scottish Terrier sitting
18cms
See 1094 – size variation
$175-$375

1079
Airedale Terrier
20.3cms
$175-$400

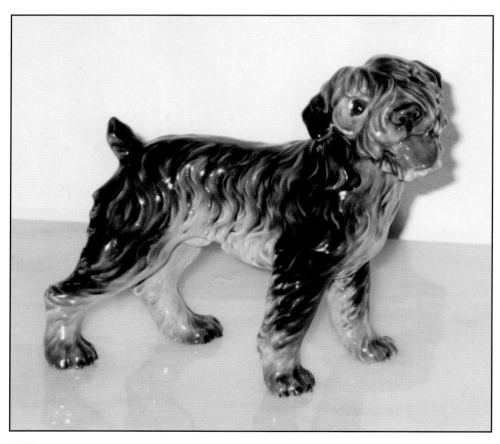

1080
Kerry Blue Terrier
15cms
$150-$275

1081
Lynx - hissing
16cms
$550-$850

1081
Lynx - bronze

1082
Greenland Hound
18cms
$175-$350

1083
Turkey cock
48cms
$1,500-$4,000

1084
German Shepherd lying
24.5cms
See 1130 – size variation
$300-$500

1085
Girl hugging Wire Haired Fox Terrier
20cms
$450-$800

1086
Monkey on rock
21cms
$300-$400

1087
German Shepherd standing
21.5cms
$300-$425

1088
French Bulldog sitting
16.5cms
See 1098 – size variation
$150-$300

1089
Dancing Girl
51cms
$1,500-$4,000

1090
Mouse dancing
7.5cms
$75-$175

1094
Scottish Terrier sitting
9.5cms
See 1078 – size variation
$125-$250

1095
Schnauzer
13cms
$175-$300

1096
Boy reading
14cms
$250-$350

1098
French Bulldog sitting
7.5cms
See 1088 – size variation
$100-$200

1100
German Shepherd
'King Tut" is impressed
on front of base
15cms
$225-$400

1101
Penguin
7.2cms
$75-$125

1102
Skye Terrier - standing
16.5cms
$175-$350

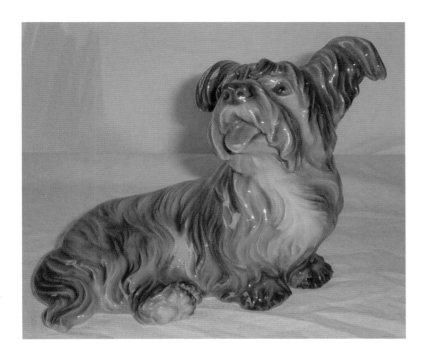

1103
Skye Terrier - sitting
15cms
$150-$325

1104
Long Eared Owl
36cms
Compare Bing & Grondahl 1846
$1,250-$2,000

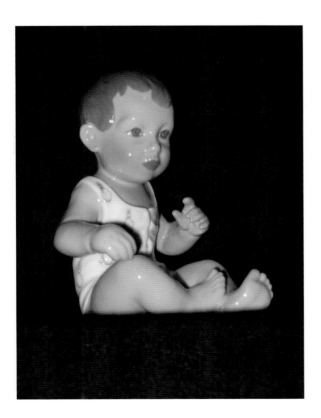

1105
Baby sitting
12cms
$200-$300

1106
Girl with doll
17.5cms
$250-$350

1107
Girl reading
21cms
$375-$525

1108
Cat
20cms
$150-$300

1109
Pekinese – book end
12cms
$175-$400

1111
Great Dane seated
26cms
$350-$600

1110
Amager girl - seated
22cms
Modelled on Christa Dahl-Jensen
$550-$800

1112
Great Dane lying
29cms
$350-$600

1111 and 1112
Great Danes seated and lying

1113
Elephant
14.5cms
$150-$250

1114
Javanese dancer
23.5cms
$550-$850

1115
Elephant
7.4cms
$75-$150

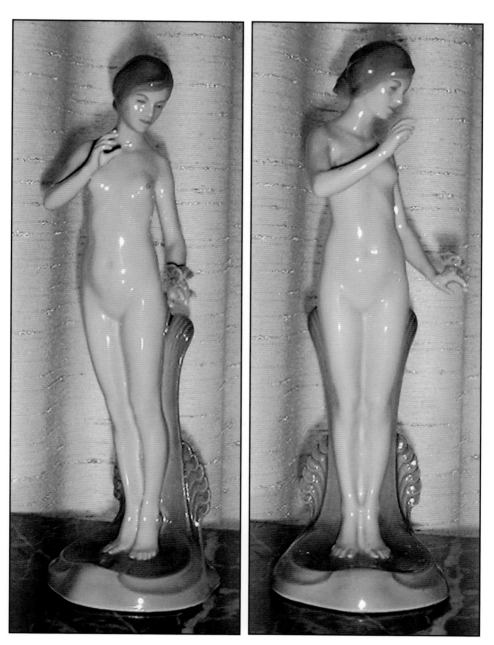

1116
Girl with a butterfly
20cms
$350-$500

1117
Girl from East - Sierra Leone
25cms
$750-$950

1118
Wire Haired Fox Terrier
9.5cms
Compare Bing & Grondahl 1998
$100-$200

1119
Woman making ceramics
11cms
$100-$200

1120
Maltese Terrier
6.5cms
$100-$175

1122
Bear on rock
9.8cms
See 1017 – size variation
$150-$250

1123
Egyptian woman
42cms
Available in blue and green
$1,500-$2,500

 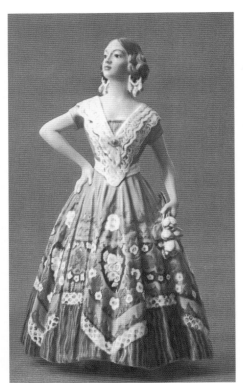 

1124
Spanish dancer
Earliest version in blue, later versions in green
25cms
$650-$900

1125
Siamese temple dancer
28.5cms
$1,500-$3,000

1128
Great Dane
13cms
$150-$350

1129
Arabian girl
42.5cms
Earliest versions in green,
later versions in blue.
Modelled on theatrical
costume.
$1,500-$2,500

1130
German Shepherd
11.5cms
See 1084 – size variation
$150-$375

1131
Dachshund
6.5cms
See 1340 – size variation
$75-$175

1132
German Shepherd - sitting
19.5cms
$250-$550

1133
Cavalier King Charles Spaniel
9.8cms
$150-$275

1134
Pekinese puppy
8.4cms
$125-$225

1135
Bulldog
10cms
Compare Bing &
Grondahl 1676
$150-$250

1136
Bali woman
21.5cms
$850-$1,250

1137
Borzoi
22cms
See 1143 – size variation
$350-$450

1138
Polar bear
12.2cms
See 1156 – size variation
$100-$200

1139
Bulldog puppy
7cms
$75-$175

1140
Hare standing
10cms
$125-$175

1141
Hare
7.5cms
$125-$175

1142
Girl from Hedebo
28.5cms
2 versions
$600-$800

1143
Borzoi
11cms
See 1137 – size variation
$100-$250

1144
Girl from Havdrup
28cms
$650-$850

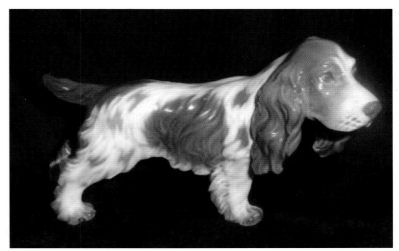

1145
Cocker Spaniel
17.5cms
See 1304 – size variation
$175-$400

1146
Pekinese
9cms
See 1337 – size variation
$100-$250

1147
Deer (doe)
17.5cms
$250-$400

1148
Pomeranian
7cms
$100-$175

1149
Cairn Terrier
14.8cms
$125-$275

1150
Girl from Skovshoved
22cms
$600-$800

1151
Girl with pail
9.5cms
$225-$325

1152
Girl with teddy
14.2cms
$350-$450

1153
Oriental flute player
24.5cms
$1,000-$1,500

1154
Man with accordion
22cms
$300-$500

1155
Geisha playing instrument
23.5cms
$500-$800

1156
Polar bear
32.5cms
See 1138 – size variation
$400-$600

1157
Polar bear - sitting
38.5cms
$450-$750

1158
Girl with Christmas goat
21cms
$450-$600

1159
Japanese woman
35cms
$1,750-$2,250

1160
'Psyche'
10cms
Blanc de chine
$75-$125

1161
Cupid with ball
10cms
Blanc de chine
$75-$125

1163
Cupid with rose
10cms
Blanc de chine
$75-$125

1164
'Cupid & Psyche'
18.5cms
Blanc de chine
$325-$425

1162
Cupid playing with foot
10cms
Blanc de chine
$75-$125

1165
Girl from Fano
18.5cms
$350-$450

1167
Boy with blocks
13.5cms
Modelled on Anker Dahl-Jensen
$275-$375

1168
Nude
18cms
Blanc de chine
$300-$450

1166
Boy with car
14cms
Modelled on Anker Dahl-Jensen
$300-$400

1169
Pekinese
37cms
$850-$1,250

1170
Boxer
21cms
$250-$350

1171
Javanese Princess
34.5cms
$2,000-$3,750

1180
Girl with snowball
19cms
$225-$400

1186
English Setter sitting
22.5cms
$375-$450

1187
English Setter lying
27.5cms
$350-$450

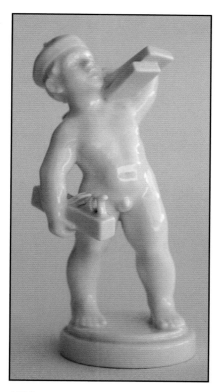

1188
Carpenter
13.5cms
Blanc de chine
$100-$200

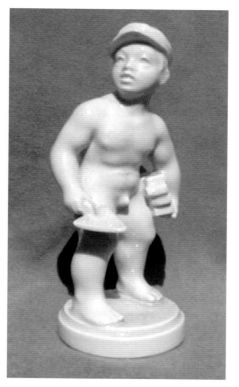

1189
Bricklayer
14cms
Blanc de chine
$100-$200

1190
Baker
13.5cms
Blanc de chine
$100-$200

1191
Blacksmith
13.5cms
Blanc de chine
$100-$200

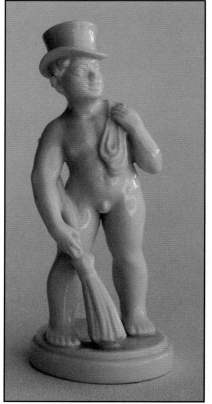

1192
Chimneysweep
15cms
Blanc de chine
$100-$200

1193
Paver (construction)
15.5cms
Blanc de chine
$100-$200

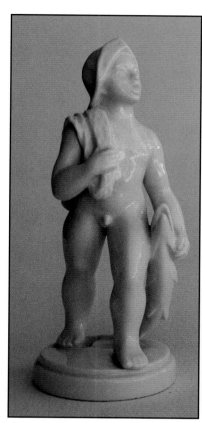

1194
Fisherman
15cms
Blanc de chine
$100-$200

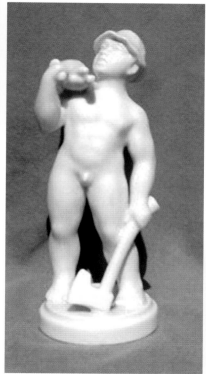

1195
Butcher
15cms
Blanc de chine
$100-$200

1196
Boy eating sausages
18.5cms
$350-$450

1197
Girl knitting
14cms
$250-$350

1204
Girl with toy elephant
16.5cms
$350-$450

1205
Boy with top
17.5cms
$350-$500

1206
Schnauzer with boy on base
27.5cms
$650-$950

1207
'Else' (Dahl-Jensen)
19cms
$350-$450

1208
Sumatra dancer
30.5cms
$850-$1,500

1209
Girl from Frederiksborg
31.5cms
$650-$1,000

1210
Girl from Aalborg
31.5cms
$650-$1,000

1211
Bust of African woman
19.5cms
$400-$575

1212
Lady reclining on chaise longue
29cms
2 versions, Modelled on a theatrical costume
$1,250-$1,750

1213
Girl with dog and bone
25cms
$650-$850

1214
Boy & girl & boat
20.5cms
$600-$800

1215
'Evening Sun'
29.5cms
$550-$750

1216
'Morning Sun'
29.5cms
$550-$850

1217
'Greta'
15.5cms
$300-$400

1219
'Hanne' - 2 versions
21cms
$375-$500

1218
Boy with trumpet
14csm
$250-$350

1220
'Proposal'
28cms
Modelled on Anker and
Christa Dahl-Jensen
$1,500-$2,000

1221
Oriental dancer
28cms
$1,250-$2,000

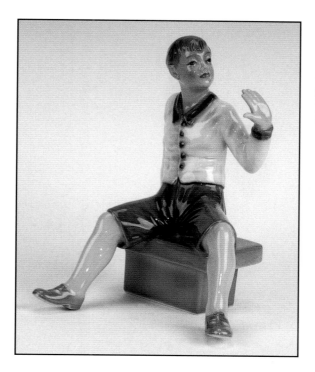

1222
Seated boy
14.5cms
$250-$375

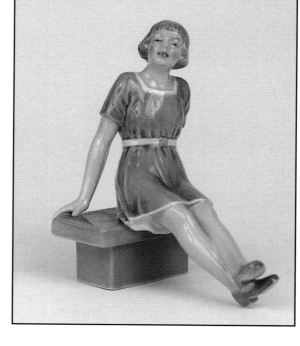

1223
Seated girl
14.5cms
$250-$375

1224
Ballerina with mirror
18.5cms
$450-$550

1225
Sailor boy
21.5cms
$325-$450

1226
Indian flame dancer
33cms
$1,500-$2,750

1228
Boy with carrot
12cms
$150-$275

1229
Indian bust
20.5cms
$500-$600

1230
Sparrow
9.5cms
$125-$225

1232
Goldfinch
10cms
Compare Bing & Grondahl 1850
$125-$225

1233
Long-tailed Tit
13.3cms
Compare Bing & Grondahl
1764
$150-$250

1234
Cow lying
20cms
$275-$375

1236
Desert Fox
12cms
$175-$275

1237
Antelope
20cms
$400-$550

1239
Kinglet
6.8cms
$100-$175

1240
Pied Flycatcher
10cms
$100-$175

1238
Oriental fruit seller
21cms
$650-$900

1241
Brambling
10cms
$100-$175

1242
Redstart
12cms
$125-$250

1243
Waxwing
14cms
$150-$250

1246
Tiger sitting
23cms
Compare Bing & Grondahl 1712
$850-$1,250

1247
Blue Warbler
11cms
$125-$260

1248
Wagtail
14.5cms
$175-$275

1249
Chaffinch
11cms
$125-$225

1250
American Kinglet
9.5cms
$125-$200

1251
Woman's head
11cms
$100-$200

1253
'Evening Prayer'
16cms
$500-$750

1254
Moroccan dancer
28cms
$1,250-$2,000

1260
Indonesian Temple Dancer
29cms
$1,250-$2,000

1268
Hawaiian girl with bird
16.5cms
$800-$1,200

1269
Madonna & Child
32cms
$1,000-$1,500

1270
Boy with mouse
13cms
$325-$425

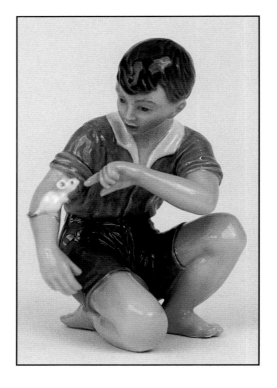

1277
'Ida'
14.5cms
$250-$350

1279
Peewit
15.5cms
$275-$375

1280
Robin
10.5cms
$150-$225

1281
Duck
8cms
Compare Bing & Grondahl 1855
$100-$150

1287
Girl with an apple basket
16.5cms
$300-$400

1288
Girl with apple branch
16cms
$300-$400

1289
'Etude'
19cms
Also available in blue
$500-$650

1291
Boy with cat
11cms
$175-$250

1292
Pompeiian dancer
27cms
$750-$1,250

1293
Spanish dancers
35.5cms
$1,500-$2,500

1294
Fisher boy
21cms
$350-$600

1295
'Bente'
14.5cms
$275-$425

1296
Goosegirl
23cms
Modelled on Else Dahl-Jensen
$700-$900

1297
Princess with fan
20.5cms
$375-$500

100

1298
Prince & Princess
23cms
$500-$800

1299
Snake charmer
21cms
$1,250-$1,750

1300
Amager boy with pipe
23.5cms
Modelled on Anker Dahl-Jensen
$750-$950

1301
Girl with vegetables
21cms
$600-$725

1305
Sudanese man with cockatoo
23cms
$850-$1,500

1304
Cocker Spaniel
14.5cms
See 1145 – size variation
$100-$200

1308
Budgerigar
11cms
$175-$250

1310
Polar bear (walking)
23.5cms
$300-$400

1309
'Flora'
25.5cms
$450-$650

1311
Kris fighter
17.5cms
$500-$700

1312
'The dream'
17.5cms
$400-$600

1314
Cuckoo
17cms
Compare Bing & Grondahl 1770
$200-$300

1315
Australian Wren
9.5cms
$125-$200

1316
Cockatoo
11cms
$125-$200

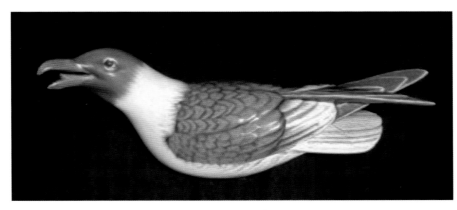

1318
Seagull
24.5cms
Compare Bing &
Grondahl 1808 and
1809
$300-$400

1319
Tern
15cms
$200-$300

1320
Warbler
9.2cms
$150-$250

1321
House Martin
12cms
$100-$250

1322
Aju Sitra (dancer)
18.8cms
$400-$600

1323
'Monuia'
15.5cms
$400-$600

1324
Bridesmaid from Fano
22.5cms
$600-$800

1325
Fano woman
32cms
$600-$800

1326
Japanese juggler
18cms
$650-$900

1327
Children with picture book
12cms
$400-$500

1328
'Ole'
14.5cms
$200-$350

1330
Ferret
10.8cms
$100-$150

1329
Cat
9.5cms
$125-$200

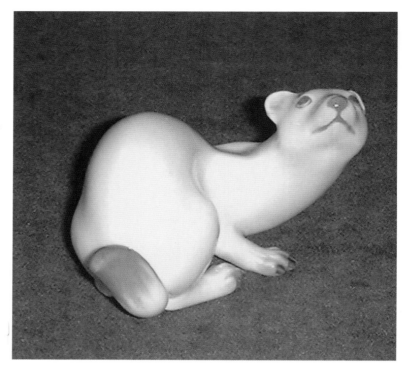

1331
Ferret
7.5cms
$100-$150

1332
'Ellen'
11.5cms
$250-$350

1333
Chamois
11cms
$200-$300

1334
Faun with oil lamp
14cms
$300-$450

1335
Ballerina
15.5cms
$300-$450

1336
Faun with wine bottle
13cms
$300-$450

1337
Pekinese
16.5cms
See 1146 – size variation
$250-$350

1338
Ballerina
38.5cms
$1,250-$2,250

1339
Polar bear cubs
15cms
$200-$300

1340
Dachshund
10.5cms
See 1131 – size variation
$175-$275

1341
Mermaid
25cms
$800-$1200

1342
Merman on rock
22.8cms
$500-$750

1343
Woodpecker
15cms
Compare Bing & Grondahl 1717
$250-$350

1344
Bear cubs
14.5cms
$275-$400

1345
Kookaburra
15.5cms
$200-$300

1346
Bear cub
10cms
$200-$300

1347
Bear cub
10cms
$175-$275

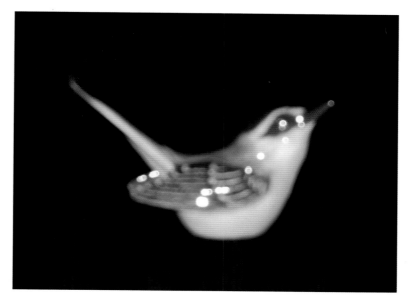

1348
Flycatcher
9cms
$100-$150

1349
Bird on a nest
15cms
$250-$350

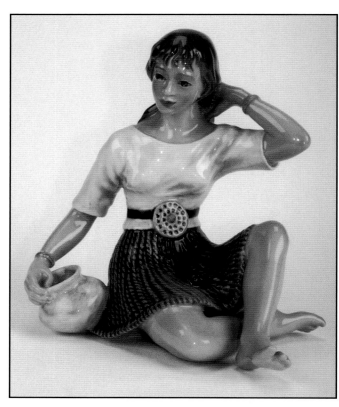

1350
Girl from Egtved (costume from the Bronze Age)
15.5cms
$400-$550

1352
Oriental dancer
21cms
$850-$1,100

1353
Girl selling pearls
13cms
$200-$350

1355
Rose breasted crossbill
13cms
$175-$250

1356
Crossbill
10.5cms
$175-$250

1357
Jay
20cms
$275-$400

1358
Greenland boy kneeling
14cms
$325-$425

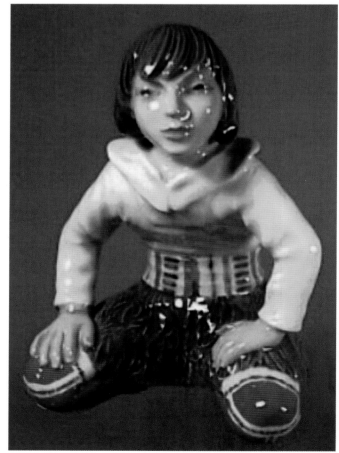

1359
Japanese girl
19cms
$500-$700

1360
Berber girl
21cms
$750-$1,000

1361
Gull
9.8cms
Compare Bing &
Grondahl 1810
$75-$125

1362
American Indian bust
19.5cms
$350-$500

1363
Geese
12cms
$100-$200

1364
Goose
11cms
$75-$125

1365
'Tine'
19cms
$300-$400

1367
Mallard
17.5cms
$250-$350

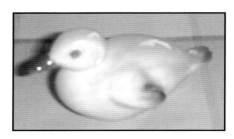

1368
Duckling
7cms
$75-$150

1369
Duckling

1375
Perch
16.5cms
$150-$250

1370
Duckling
7cms
$75-$150

1371
Duckling

1372
Duckling

1376
Sea Roach
17cms
See 1385 - size variation
$200-$300

1377
Sea Scorpion
17cms
$175-$275

1378
Schoolgirl from Sweden
18cms
$300-$400

1380
Sea lion
18.5cms
$350-$450

1381
Seal
20cms
$300-$400

1382
Sprat
12cms
$75-$125

1383
Crucian Carp
15cms
$200-$300

1384
Redfish
13cms
$75-$150

1385
Sea Roach
13.5cms
See 1376 - size variation
$100-$200

1386
Great Redfish
23cms
$250-$400

1388
Codfish
25cms
$400-$475

Illustrated Numerical List of Figurines by Other Sculptors

In this chapter the figures by sculptors other than Jens Peter Dahl-Jensen are listed in numerical order.

Herman Andersen

1174
Girl with apple
28cms
Blanc de chine
$350-$450

Vilhelm Andersen

1121
Ermine on log
23cms
$200-$350

Carl Johan Bonnesen

1055
Chimpanzee
14cms
$200-$275

1056
Elephant - African
29.5cms
$850-$1,250

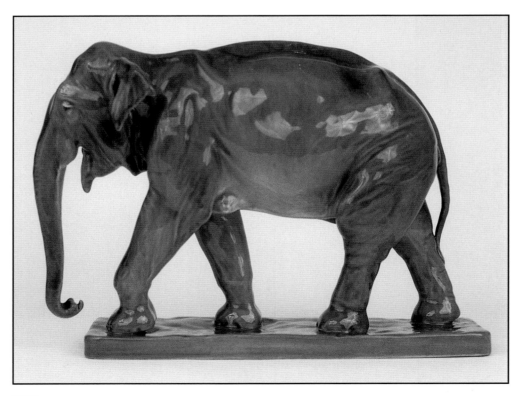

1057
Elephant - Indian
27.5cms
$850-$1,250

1059
Elephant with calf
33cms
$1,000-$1,600

1060
Bear lying on back with 2 cubs playing
22.5cms
$350-$500

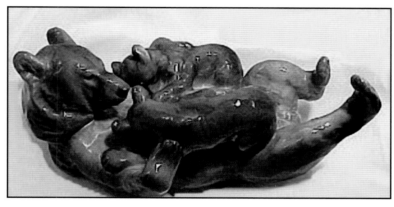

1067
Polar bear
19cms
$300-$450

1068
Polar bear & cubs
19.5cms
Compare Royal Copenhagen 321
$300-$450

1126
Polar bear
23cms
Compare Royal Copenhagen 321
$275-$375

1127
Cat sitting
18cms
$300-$400

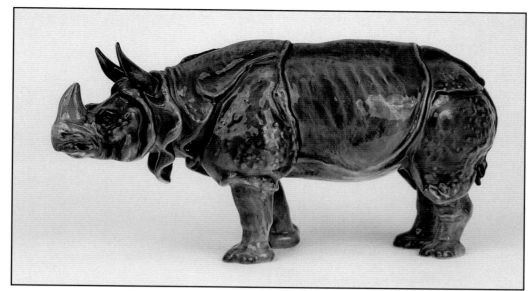

1231
Rhinoceros
30.5cms
$700-$900

1252
French workhorse
31.5cms
Compare Royal Copenhagen 471
$1,250-$1,750

Jens Jakob Bregno

1172
Girl with mandolin
18cms
$300-$400

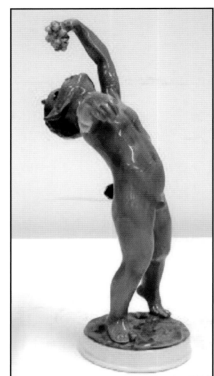

1173
Faun with grapes
18.5cms
$300-$550

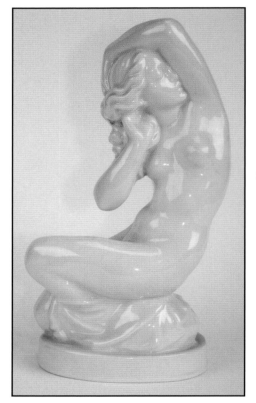

1175
'Spring'
20cms
Blanc de chine
$250-$450

1176
Faun & woman
19cms
Blanc de chine
$450-$600

1177
'Morning'
25cms
$500-$675

1178
'Eva '
20cms
Blanc de chine
$250-$500

1179
'Hercules'
20cms
Blanc de chine
$250-$500

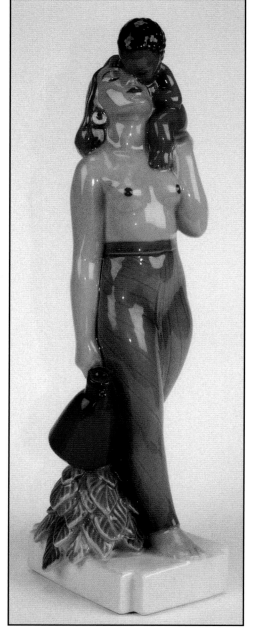

1181
Mother & baby
31.5cms
$450-$550

1182
'Susanne'
9cms
Blanc de chine
$100-$200

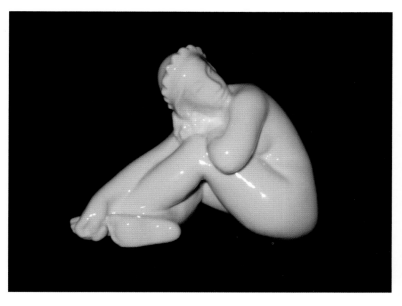

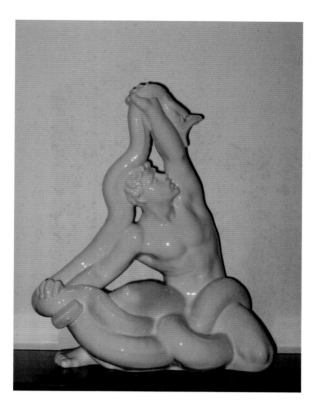

1183
'Thor'
25cms
Blanc de chine
$500-$750

1184
'Paradise'
25cms
Blanc de chine
$500-$700

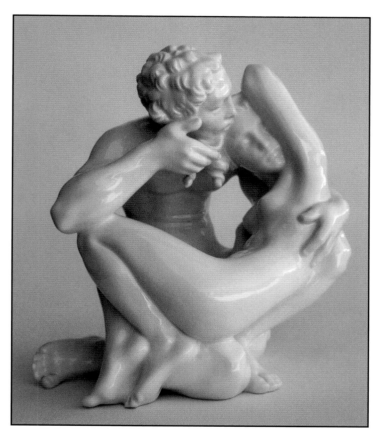

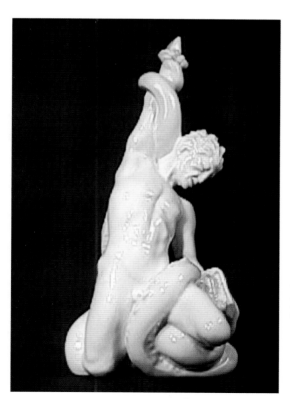

1185
'Thor'
Blanc de chine
$150-$250

1198
Faun with ducklings
24.5cms
$750-$1,250

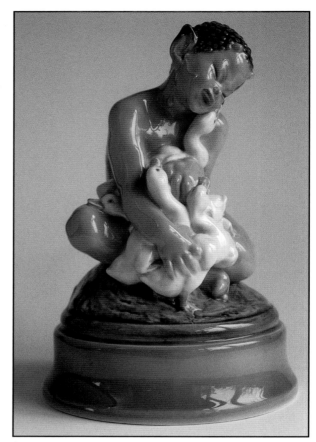

1199
'The Elevation'
Blanc de chine
$75-$150

1200
'Susanne's Sister'
11cms
Blanc de chine
$75-$150

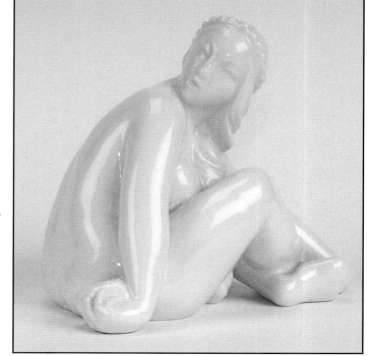

1201
'Jacob's Fight'
16.5cms
Blanc de chine
$300-$550

1202
Adam and Eve
Blanc de chine

Georg Christensen

1091
Chinese on pillow
9cms
$150-$250

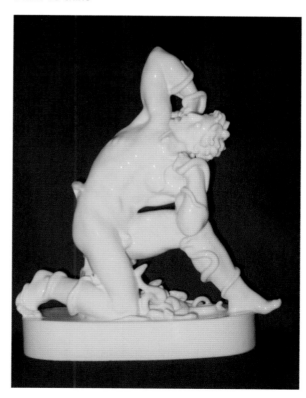

1203
'Regnar Lodbrog'
30cms
Blanc de chine
$500-$900

1092
Mermaid
8.5cms
$100-$175

1093
Girl on stool
8.2cms
$100-$200

Helge Dorlit

1374
Fawn
7cms
$75-$125

1373
Hunter with dog
24cms
$500-$800

1389
Perched Owl
17cms
Compare Bing & Grondahl 1800
$250-$350

Johan Galster

1390
Snowy Owl
43cms
$1,500-$2,000

1392
'Lisa'
14.5cms
$375-$475

Lauritz Jensen

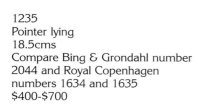

1235
Pointer lying
18.5cms
Compare Bing & Grondahl number
2044 and Royal Copenhagen
numbers 1634 and 1635
$400-$700

1244
Sculptor (self portrait)
20cms
$400-$675

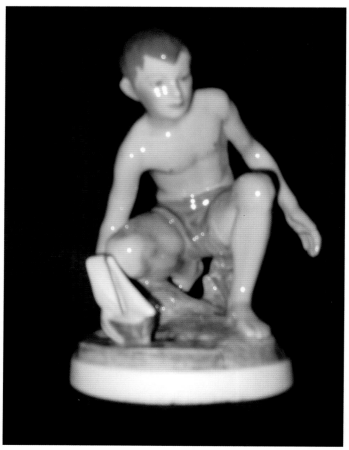

1245
Boy with sail boat
14.5cms
$250-$350

1255
Broholmer puppy
17cms
$350-$500

1256
Buffalo lying
28.5cms
$600-$900

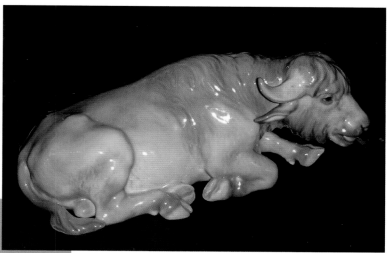

1257
Dachshunds playing
20cms
$600-$1,000

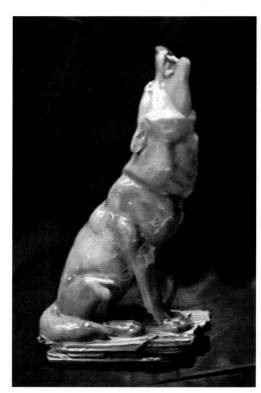

1258
Wolf howling
22.5cms
$250-$350

1259
Lion & lioness
33cms
Compare Bing & Grondahl 2279
$750-$1,000

1261
American Indian on horse
37.5cms
$1,500-$2,500

1262
Girl with cow
20cms
$750-$1,000

1263
Lion roaring
40cms
$1,500-$2,000

1264
Friesian bull
29cms
See 1302 – size variation
$700-$950

1265
Deer
23cms
$300-$400

1266
Cowboy on horse
41.5cms
$1,500-$2,500

1267
Deer with fawn
27cms
$1,250-$1,750

1271
Wounded soldier with a horse
25cms
$1000-$1,750

1272
Polar bear with fish
18cms
$300-$500

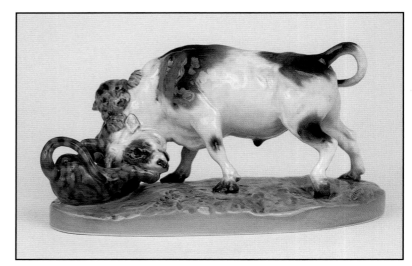

1273
Bull goring tiger
28cms
$550-$800

1274
Lion cubs - pair
31.5cms
$700-$1,000

1275
Lion cub
15cms
$350-$450

1276
Woman with fawn (on base)
16cms
$500-$750

1278
English Setters on base
40cms
$1,000-$1,500

1282
Irish Setter on base
31.5cms
$750-$1,000

1283
German Shorthair Pointer on base
24.7cms
$500-$850

1284
Refugees
23cms
$400-$600

1285
Tiger with haunch
24.5cms
Compare Bing & Grondahl
1712, 2056 and Royal
Copenhagen 714
$550-$800

1286
Lion roaring
20cms
Compare Bing & Grondahl 1793
$450-$600

1290
Osprey with fish
20.5cms
$500-$800

1302
Friesian bull
21cms
See 1264 – size variation
$550-$800

1391
Bull
20.5cms
$425-$600

Borge Jorgensen

1351
'Lene'
11cms
$200-$300

1354
'Jette'
10.5cms
$200-$300

1366
'Anne'
13.8cms
$325-$425

Poul Lemser

1034
'Venus & Cupid'
20cms
Blanc de chine
$275-$325

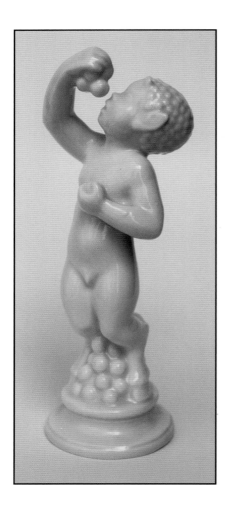

1035
Faun with grapes
15cms
Blanc de chine
$125-$200

1037
'Leda & Swan'
22.5cms
Blanc de chine
$350-$500

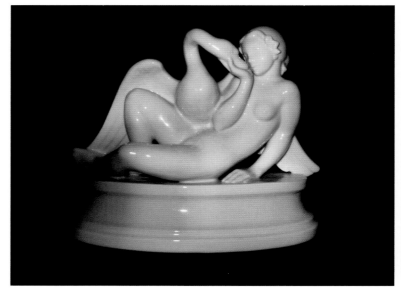

1038
Faun with baby
13cms
Blanc de chine
$125-$200

1039
Faun & nymph
27.5cms
Blanc de chine
$350-$550

1042
Bonbon dish with figurine
12cms
Blanc de chine
$250-$400

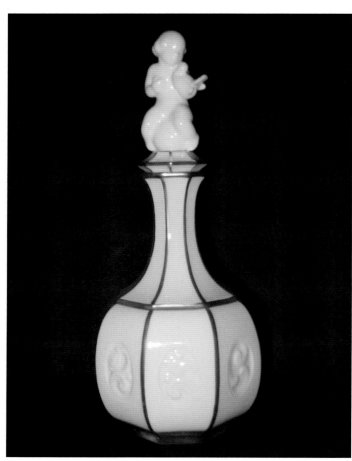

1043
Bottle with figurine
15cms
Blanc de chine
$250-$400

1044
Little girl with pigeon
11cms
Blanc de chine
$150-$250

1046
Boy with duck
11cms
Blanc de chine
$150-$250

1070
'Hans Clodhopper'
22.5cms
$400-$600

1071
'Emperor's New Clothes'
23.5cms
$450-$700

Aug. Svejstrup Madsen

1045
Rabbit
17cms
Also available in Cracquelé
Compare Bing & Grondahl 1597 and 1599
$225-$400

1054
Duckling
12.7cms
Compare Bing & Grondahl 1588 and 1589
$125-$200

1073
Penguin
21.5cms
Compare Bing & Grondahl 1821
$300-$425

Emma Mathiesen

1097
Choirboy
20.5cms
$250-$350

1379
Salmon
23cms
Compare Bing & Grondahl 2366
$275-$400

1387
Trout
19cms
Compare Bing & Grondahl 2366
$250-$350

Patrick Nordstrom

1047
Girl with fish
22cms
Blanc de chine
$450-$800

Inger Osterbye

1227
Greenlander with baby
26.5cms
$900-$1,250

Linda Roerup

1303
Brother & sister
16cms
$300-$400

1306
Girl with roller-skates
13cms
$350-$450

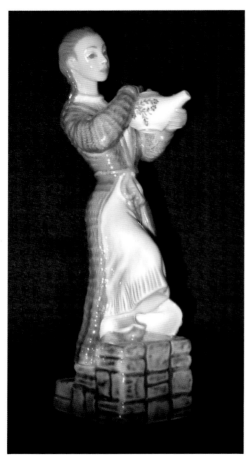

1307
Tea girl
22cms
$400-$650

1313
Woman with 3 pigs
14.5cms
$400-$500

1317
Gypsy woman
12cms
$300-$550

Viola Wahlstedt

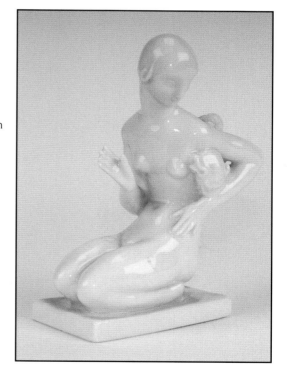

1016
Woman with fish
12cms
Blanc de chine
$200-$325

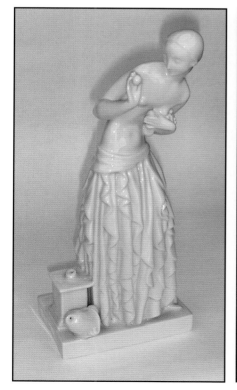

1023
Pomona
27cms
Blanc de chine
NB. Broken flowerpot in lefthand photo—this piece was sold as a third.
$300-$425

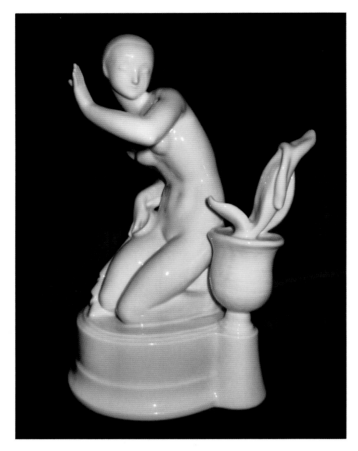

1033
Woman with agave
24.5cms
Blanc de chine
$250-$350

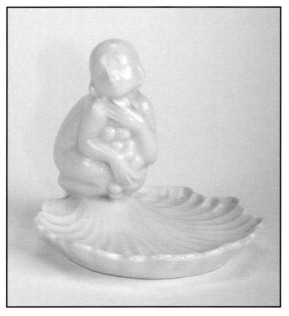

1099
Girl on a shell
8cms
Both underglaze and blanc de chine
$50-$175

Illustrated Numerical List
of Non-figurative Work

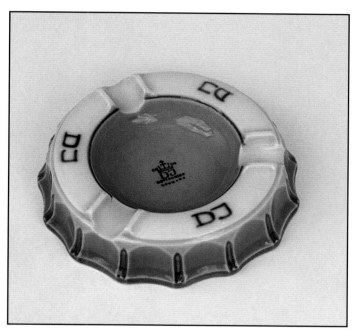

Ashtray

14 Bowl

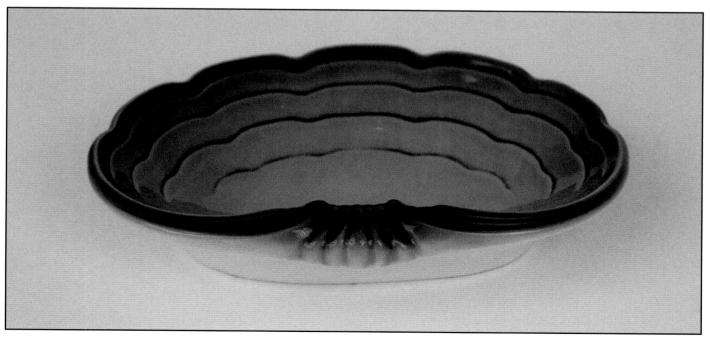

84 Shell dish

157 Vase
30cms

Vase and mark

87a Pigmy Hippo – test piece?

Illustrated Numerical List of Figurines Sculpted by Dahl-Jensen for the Bing & Grondahl Factory, 1897-1925

If applicable, a modern Royal Copenhagen number is included to indicate that the piece is still in production.

Rating – this is very subjective, based on experience of the world market and trends in value and demand.

*   In production by Royal Copenhagen.

**   Piece not in production, easily obtainable.

***   Piece not in production and sometimes difficult to find.

****   Rare and/or older pieces but with limited appeal.

*****   Rare, highly desirable subject matter.

If a piece is still in production under the Royal Copenhagen mark, the MSRP figure is the 'new' cost in the United States at December, 2001. Stoneware has not been valued as the market is smaller and less reliable information is available.

1000
Fish-shaped covered dish

1500
Snowy Owl
44cms
**

In production 1988
$550-800

1502
Elephant on knees
29cms
***
$400-650

1510
Monkey looking at tortoise
13cms
**

Also available in stoneware.
In production 1984
$125-225

1512
Hippopotamus
34cms
*****
$750-1000

1515
Woman standing
24cms
****
$125-225

1525
Woman
27cms
****

Also produced as lamp base
$300-400

1531
Falcon
38cms
**

In production 1984
$700-1000

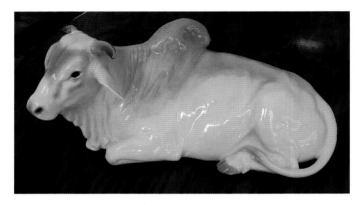

1547
Brahma Bull
38cms
*****
$750-950

1545
Monkey looking at tortoise
34cms
****

In production 1984
$1250-2000

1548
Duck
Compare Dahl-Jensen 1029
8cms
**

In production 1988
$40-60

1553
Kitten sitting
10cms
**
In production 1972
$225-325

1559
Guinea pigs – three
12cms
*****
$350-450

1562
Mice - pair on dish
Compare Dahl-Jensen 1011
14cms
*****
$250-400

1566
Mice – pair
7cms
*****
$125-225

1572
Fox curled
17cms
*****
$150-350

1582
RC number 405
Pig sitting
12cms
*
$75-125

1583
Sow with 8 piglets
28cms
*****
$600-750

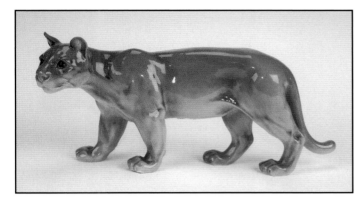

1584
Puma
Compare Dahl-Jensen 1019
26cms
****
$500-800

1588
Duckling
Compare Dahl-Jensen 1054
10cms
***
$40-100

1589
Duckling
Compare Dahl-Jensen 1054
11cms
***
$50-125

1596
Rabbit - lop eared
11cms
***
$75-125

1597
Rabbit – grooming
Compare Dahl-Jensen 1045
11cms
***
$75-125

1599
Rabbit
Compare Dahl-Jensen 1045
9cms
***
$75-125

1605
Bulldog
24cms
*****
With tail
$350-500

1610
Magpie
33cms
****
$100-175

1613
Jaguar
Compare Dahl-Jensen 1020
47cms
***
$500-850

1615
Horse
26cms
*****
$350-450

1619
RC number 407
Kingfisher
Compare Dahl-Jensen 1049
11cms
*
Also available in stoneware
$75-150
MSRP
$145

1623
Dish with bird on lid
12cms
**
In production 1984
$100-200

1626
Tapir
25cms
****
$250-500

1629
RC number 409
Polar bear sitting
19cms
*
$75-125
MSRP
$195

1628
Peacock
40cms
**
1984
$500-650

1630
Pekinese puppies - pair
15cms
****
$300-500

1631
Pekinese sitting
Compare Dahl-Jensen 1003
9cms
***
$100-200

1635
RC number 411
'Pessimist' - titmouse
13cms
*
Also available in stoneware
$75-125
MSRP
$115

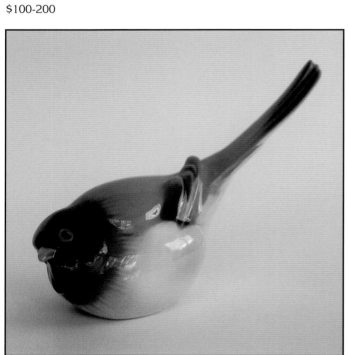

1633
RC number 410
'Optimist' - titmouse
13cms
*
Also available in stoneware
$75-125
MSRP
$115

1637
Pekinese puppy sitting
Compare Dahl-Jensen 1003
16cms
***
$350-450

1663
Collie lying
29cms
***
$350-550

1666
Hawk
26cms
**
In production 1984
$400-600

1670
RC number 415
'Protection'
18cms
*
Also available in stoneware
$100-200
MSRP
$275

1675
Crested Tit
Compare Dahl-Jensen 1050
9cms
**
In production 1984
$75-125

1699
Goat
17cms
**
Also available in stoneware. In production 1984
$75-150

1676
Bulldog
Compare Dahl-Jensen 1135
11cms
**
In production 1984
$75-175

1700
Goat
16cms
**
Also available in stoneware.   In production 1984
$75-150

1708
Finch group
12cms
**
In production 1988
$75-125

1707
Finch
11cms
**
In production 1984
$50-100

1714
Crow
33cms
**
Also available in stoneware. In production 1984
$125-225

1717
Woodpecker
Compare Dahl-Jensen 1343
19cms
**
In production 1984
$75-175

1728
RC number 419
Mouse – white
Compare Dahl-Jensen 1010
5cms
*
See 1801
$30-60
MSRP
$65

1722
Squirrel
17cms
*****
$250-450

1725
Seagull with fish
37cms
**
In production 1988
$100-200

1744
RC number 420
Blackcock (Black grouse)
41cms
*
$700-850

1752
Dachshund
19cms
***
$150-300

1764
Wagtail
Compare Dahl-Jensen 1233 and 1248
14cms
**
In production 1984
$75-150

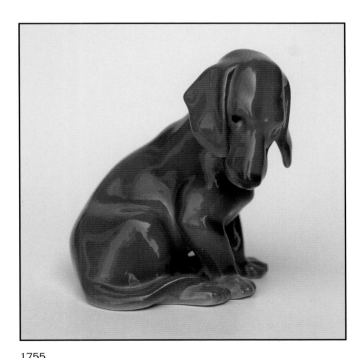

1755
Dachshund
7cms
**
In production 1984
$50-150

1770
RC number 423
Cuckoo
Compare Dahl-Jensen 1314
24cms
*
Stoneware
$150-300
MSRP
$495

1775
Swallow
14cms
**
Also available in stoneware. In production 1984
$75-150

1784
Silver pheasant
43cms
**
In production 1988
$700-850

1776
Flycatcher
10cms
**
In production 1984
$75-125

1795
Eagle - golden
51cms
**
In production 1988
$1750-2750

1801
Mouse gray
Compare Dahl-Jensen 1010
5cms
**
See 1728. In production 1988
$30-70

1800
Owl
Compare Dahl-Jensen 1389
11cms
**
In production 1988
$50-100

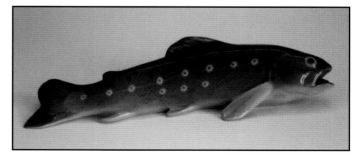

1803
Trout
22cms
**
In production 1984
$75-125

1805
Dachshunds - pair
10cms
***
$150-200

1808
RC number 428
Gull with fish
Compare Dahl-Jensen 1318
14cms
*
$50-125
MSRP
$90

1809
RC number 429
Gull crying
Compare Dahl-Jensen 1318
9cms
*
$50-125
MSRP
$75

1810
RC number 430
Gull
Compare Dahl-Jensen 1361
9cms
*
$50-125
MSRP
$75

1833
Rabbit
11cms
***
$75-125

1844
Cat
30cms
*****
$200-300

1850
Goldfinch
Compare Dahl-Jensen 1232
8cms
**
In production 1984
$75-125

1846
Owl on base
Compare Dahl-Jensen 1104
51cms
***
$2000-3000

1855
Tufted duck
Compare Dahl-Jensen 1281
10cms
**
Also available in stoneware. In production 1988
$50-100

1869
Sparrow with young
15cms
**
In production 1988
$100-200

1986
Pekinese sitting
Compare Dahl-Jensen 1003
5.5cms
***
$75-125

1987
Pekinese
Compare Dahl-Jensen 1003
5.5cms
***
$75-125

1993
Mountain Lion
Compare Dahl-Jensen 1019
13cms
****
$450-650

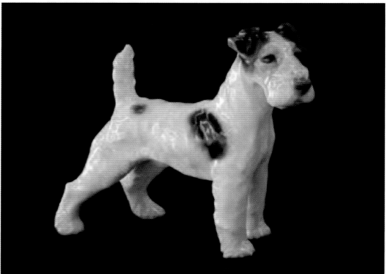

1998
Terrier
Compare Dahl-Jensen 1001 and 1118
17cms
**
In production 1984
$150-300

2000
French Bull Terrier
12.5cms
***
$300-500

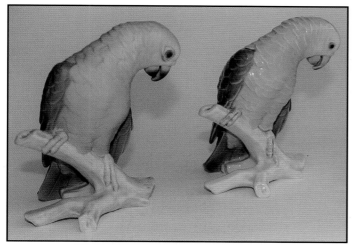

2019
Parrot
14cms
**
Also available in stoneware. In production 1988
$125-250

2027
Sealyham puppy
Compare Dahl-Jensen 1008
10cms
**

In production 1984
$75-175

2028
Sealyham puppy
Compare Dahl-Jensen 1008
10cms
**

In production 1984
$75-150

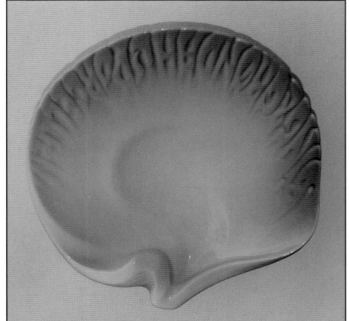

Oil lamp
Dahl-Jensen

Bibliography

Bing, Harald, *Bing & Grondahls Porcelaensfabrik 1853 – 1928* Copenhagen: 1928

Bing & Grondahls Porcellainfabrik Kjobenhavn 1890 Copenhagen: 1890

Brohan-Museum, *Porzellan Kunst und Design 1889 bis 1939* , Berlin: 1993

Dahl-Jensen, *Georg Dahl-Jensen*

Grandjean, Bredo L. *Kongelig dansk Porcelain 1884-1980,* Denmark: 1983

Jakobsen, Gunnar, *Dansk Keramisk Bibliografi 1880-1997* Host & Son

Lassen, Erik, *En Kobenhavensk porcelaensfabriks historie,* Denmark: Nyt Nordisk Forlag Arnold Busck A/S 1978

Museum fur Angewandte Kunst - Koln, *Kopenhagener Porzellan und Steinzeug,* Cologne: 1991

Royal Copenhagen Porcelain 1777-2000, Copenhagen: Nyt Nordisk Forlag Arnold Busck A/S and the authors, 2000

Vingedal, S E, *Porslinsmarken,* Forum, 1986

Dahl-Jensen made a range of shell shaped dishes for Bing & Grondahl

191

Index